Instagram – The new Facebook, Boosting your Business with Instagram Marketing

© Copyright: 2018

Jennifer Hauser

1st edition

ISBN: 9781980669050

Self-published

Print: Amazon Media EU S.à.r.l., 5 Rue Plaetis, L-2338, Luxembourg

The work including its parts is protected by copyright. Any use is prohibited without the consent of the publisher and the author. This applies to electronic or other duplication, translation, distribution and public disclosure.

Table of Contents

Table of Contents 3
Introduction 7
Chapter 1: What is Instagram? 10
   How It Works 11
      Account Creation 11
      The profile 12
      Accessing Images from other Users 12
      Interactions on Instagram 13
      Posting Photos 14
      Editing the Photos 15
      Sharing Posts 15
      Instagram Stories 16
      Hashtags 17
Chapter 2: How Instagram Works; The different functionalities 18
   Instagram Features 18
      1. Instagram Stories 19
      2. Live videos 20
      3. Instagram Algorithm 21
      4. Instagram Collections 22
   Managing your Account 24
      Photos you are tagged in 24
      Push Notifications 24
      Publishing Images and videos 25
   Multiple Instagram accounts 28

Chapter 3: How to Use Instagram for Marketing and to Earn Money 30

How to Make Money on Instagram 31
Grow your following 31
Have great quality content 31
Make use of shout-outs from other accounts 32
Be Consistent 33
Use Hashtags 33
Find Brands to Partner with 33
Where to look 34
Ways of earning Revenue 35

Tips to earn well on Instagram 36
Use hashtags effectively 36
Buying Followers 37

How to Use Instagram for Marketing 38
Maximize the use of hashtags 38
General hashtags 39
Content hashtags 39
Brand hashtags 39
Build and be involved in an Instagram Community 40
Use Sponsored Ads 41
Keep Track of your Metrics 42
Follower Growth 42
Engagement rate 42
Click through rate of URLs 43
Partner with Influencers 43
Hold Contests 44
Consider User-submitted photos 44
Be consistent in your posts 45

Chapter 4: Instagram Success Stories 47
  Anish Bhatt 47
  Reebok 50
  J Crew 51
  @spjeweler 58
  Hunter Vought 59
  Pacific Northwest Wonderland 60
  E! News 62
Chapter 5: Importance of Instagram for Online Business Success 63
  Benefits of using Instagram for marketing 63
    Visual appeal 63
    Large Audience 64
    More Engagement 65
    Storytelling Ability 66
    Keep Tabs on Competition 66
    Free Marketing from users 67
  Tips for successful Instagram marketing 67
    Having a Great Profile 67
    Offering excellent quality Content 68
    Being Consistent 68
    Increasing User Engagement 69
    Influencer Marketing 70
    Utilizing Instagram Ads 70
Conclusion 72

5

Introduction

You may have come across or heard the phrase 'one for the gram' several times the past couple of years. It is all the rage today in the world of social networking.

Everybody wants to share their lives in the form of pictures and videos with others. From trips you have taken to people you have met, there is very little that one cannot post on social media from their day to day lives.

The number of people at any given time on their smartphones or computers is remarkably high. Just look around you. Chances are, there is somebody nearby using a laptop or smartphone right now.

People join social media to connect with friends and family, among other things. Instagram especially ranks quite high in social media use, with its ease of use and access for anybody with a good internet connection.

Instagram is also quite appealing to people as they can share photos and images, making memories, and having a place to see what friends and family are up to. This makes it a popular platform to share.

The potential of this site is quite impressive, with its ability to cut across geographic locations and reach many people at once. Therefore, we bring you this book.

Imagine the opportunities it holds for you and your business; all the people waiting for you to show them what you offer.

Instagram avails a ready market for your product or service. The millions of Instagram users today are an audience to which you can make your pitch, market your product or service. Furthermore, they also make up potential clients for immediate and future sales.

To be able to tap into this platform, use it to your business' advantage, would be the move that takes your business to the next level. Instagram has become an essential platform for you to further your marketing campaigns.

Whether you are an online marketer or a business owner, this is the place to find what you have been looking for; a way to revolutionize your marketing strategy.

Sometimes all you need is to show your brand to an audience and have it stick to their minds. They need to remember it, go back to it when they need a product or service you offer.

Instagram gives you this ability to do just that, have your brand seen by a ready audience and if you do it right, it should remain in their memories.

We will take you through the whole concept of Instagram marketing from the very basics. If Instagram is new to you, worry not as we have got you covered as well, with a whole chapter explaining what it is and what it is all about.

You will learn how it works, the different tools used, and more importantly how to use it to your advantage as a business person or online marketer.

Learn how to make money through Instagram marketing, with clear strategies that we have outlined in the book. Join the world of Instagram marketers where the opportunities to be successful are endless.

Unlock your potential to be a great marketer with the tips you will get from here.

Have you already embraced Instagram marketing? If not, then this is the time to do so. Even if you are already on Instagram, you will find some great insights here to help drive your online marketing.

Read on to find out more.

Chapter 1: What is Instagram?

For a while now, Instagram has been gaining traction. Everyone is talking about it, and its use is the in thing today, together with other networks like Snapchat and Twitter. It currently has over 800 million users all over the world. You must have at one point heard of it and may be wondering what it is all about.

Instagram is a photo album of sorts. Think of the time you went over to a friend's place and their family members pulled out a photo album from years back, and you could go through it to see their memories from that time. Those moments in life that you want to capture and show your friends, adding it to your album.

It is a social networking app whose sole purpose is to allow people to share images and videos from a smartphone. You get a virtual photo album to share with friends and family. They can view your photos when you post them, and even comment about them on the app.

The app is available for use on mobile devices and computers although it works best with mobile devices. You can simply download it for free from the App Store for iOS, Google Play Store for Android devices and Windows Phone Store for phones using the Windows OS.

If you are new to Instagram, it may look like rocket science with all the icons on it. Far from this, however, you will come to find that it is easy to use once you get the hang of it.

How It Works

The first step in using Instagram is to download the app on the respective platform depending on the kind of device you are using.

Account Creation

You will need to create an account as the first step. To create your account, open the app on your mobile device and tap on the Sign-Up option. You will be prompted to enter your email address.

There is also the option of signing up with your Facebook account so that they are connected. It is on the same sign-up page, where you can either sign up or Log in with Facebook.

Once that is done, move on to the next step of creating passwords and a username. The username is what people will see when they see your posts. It usually appears on top of your post and your profile.

The username is the mode of recognition for Instagram users and is usually preceded by a symbol @. So, if you decide to name your account Greg17, it will look like this: @Greg17.

If you are opening a business account, go to settings on the app and select a business account. It will allow you to add more information such as a phone number for those who want to reach you, business hours and an address, all to make it easier to find your store and interact with you.

The profile

Once you have created your account successfully, the next step is to set up your profile. This includes choosing a suitable profile photo which will represent you, adding your name and a small message that describes you, also referred to as a bio. You can also add a link to a website if you have one.

This part is important for businesses as it gives the audience more information about you and what you offer. It also helps to get more people to follow you as they will know a bit about you. For the profile photo, think of having your company logo to market your brand.

Once this step is done, you are officially a member of Instagram and can start right away viewing images of other members as well as following them and having them follow you back. You can always change the image and update information on your profile later.

Accessing Images from other Users

To be able to see images of friends and family, you will need to follow them. Simply search for their usernames and click on the follow button beside or below the names. Instagram also may give you a list of people you may know, and you can follow them too.

People will also be able to follow you to see images that you post. On your profile, you will see the following count, showing the number of people following you as well as the number of people you are following.

There is also a privacy setting that only allows those who follow you to see your images. If you come across the profile of an individual who has the privacy setting, you will not be able to view their images and videos until you follow them.

You can set your account private or let it be open to the public according to your preferences. Having a private account lets you decide who you want to follow you as you can either accept or deny their request to follow you.

Interactions on Instagram

The app allows you to interact with others quite easily. You will have a profile and a newsfeed. On the profile, you will find information about you and the images and videos you have shared.

The newsfeed is where you will see posts by others that appear on a timeline. You can scroll to view images by other people. Here is where the interactions between you and the others occur. You can leave a comment on the images you view and like them.

You like a post by tapping on the heart shape on the bottom left corner of the image. Alternatively, you can double tap the image. It is quite a fun and interesting way to interact, as you can have conversations in the comment section.

It is easy, right?

Posting Photos

Click on the icon with a plus sign. This is where you choose photos to add on to your profile. You can either capture a photo or choose one from your device. Remember to pick a photo that is appealing and relevant.

Your account should look inviting to capture the interest of users and add them to your followers' list, so pick presentable photos that make this possible.

You will notice that you will not be attracted to users whose profiles are dull, thus you need to keep it interesting and creative.

The frequency of posting photos depends on the time you have, as well as the purpose of your posts. You can post as many times as you want since there are no limits to the number of images one can post.

Not posting for extended periods of time may, however, make it hard to increase your following. Try to post occasionally, to be relevant to other users.

Editing the Photos

Why does everyone look like a professional photographer on Instagram? You may wonder. Are they just very photogenic? Or did they all go to photography school? Well, maybe it's the good lighting. But, chances are they may have only been making effective use of the editing features offered on Instagram.

Once you choose a photo to post, you can click on the edit option where you can tweak the photo to your desires, by cropping it, trying out different filters to find which suits you most and make other adjustments as you will.

The editing tools allow you to alter contrasts, have varying degrees of brightness, change the angle of your photos or even add some blur to part of the image to make it more interesting. You can also try out different effects on the image. Discover your creativity with these changes and filters and find out how good your skills are.

Sharing Posts

Once you are satisfied with the chosen image or video, you can move to the next step. You are given the option of adding a caption to the image, tag friends, if they appear on the image or if you would like for them to be notified of it. You can also tag it to the geographic location it was taken or where you are at that moment and publish it.

Publishing means that it has been added to your profile, and it will appear on the newsfeeds of other users. They will also be able to like the image and leave comments on it.

There is the option of connecting your account with your other accounts on Facebook, Twitter, and the others, found in the configuration settings. Once you enable the settings, your images will be posted simultaneously on all the platforms you choose.

Instagram Stories

This feature was introduced to Instagram recently. You can add videos and images to your story just as a normal Instagram post. However, the images and videos posted on your story usually disappear after 24 hours.

They also do not appear on your profile. The stories usually appear on top of your Instagram feed. You can tell them apart from regular newsfeeds as the ones that appear in small photo bubbles of people you follow.

Currently, Instagram stories do not have the option for one to like or comment on them. You can only view them.

Hashtags

You cannot speak on Instagram without mentioning hashtags. These usually assist users to discover posts on an area of interest for them. For instance, for a post about baking items, you can use the hashtag #Cake or #bakers. If you go to the explore section, you can search for a specific hashtag and it will bring you posts made with that hashtag.

For a business account, this part would be important to put you on the map for users in search of something in your field.

Instagram is a fun app that lets you view amazing images. You can never see everything on, with so many images being shared around. To find new images that interest you, just head on to the explore section and type in # followed by something that you would like to see.

You can also discover new people that you may follow by tapping on the search icon represented by a magnifying glass. This takes you to posts by users like those you follow and posts you have liked before.

Instagram is all about the visuals, catering to your sense of sight. If you are one who loves visuals, then you will love the app with its ability to bring to you, art in different forms. It allows for communication and the exchange of ideas through the posts.

That is all there is to it. It is quite easy and straightforward to learn and interesting when you can use it. You will understand why people, especially the younger generation spend hours on it.

Chapter 2: How Instagram Works; The different functionalities

Now, we have a better understanding of what Instagram really is and what it is all about. With that information, we should be able to confidently use the app as marketers or business owners.

Whatever niche you are in, you can always use the app to market your product.

So, how does it work?

We have mentioned a few of the features in the previous chapter. We will then delve deeper into the different functionalities of the app and examine how the unique features work and how you may use them effectively for Instagram marketing.

If you have been interested in using Instagram for your marketing purposes but have no idea where to start, here is your chance. Let us break down the app for you in such a way that you understand it.

Instagram Features

There are several features on Instagram that you should know of to be able to use it well in marketing. It would be good to note that Instagram keeps changing with the times.

This means that the layout as well as how it works may change, with newer ideas coming into play as the team behind Instagram works to upgrade the app and keep it relevant.

Let us look at some of the current features:

1. Instagram Stories

As previously discussed in Chapter 1, Instagram Stories is one feature that was introduced recently. It lets the user add photos or videos which usually last for 24 hours.

This feature is like Snapchat as the photos and videos posted there also tend to disappear after 24 hours.

Once you open the app on your mobile device, you will see bubbles or circles at the top of your newsfeed. These are the stories posted by people you follow.

You are not limited to viewing the posts once, but you can view them over and over until the 24 hours are up after which they vanish.

You can view an image for 10 seconds before the next image on the story pops up. Tapping on the image and holding allows you to view it for a while longer.

The feature lets you record live videos to post and add as many photos as you would like to the story. Try it out, take an image or two of your products and add them to your story. This is a great way to promote your product using the feature.

Add relevant information to the image, possibly a geotag to show the viewers the location of the physical store if there is one.

There is a count for your story that shows you the number of views, that way you can know how many people see your story, and know which stories have more viewers than the others. This helps in future as you will understand what the viewers like. You also have the freedom to hide your story from some users, such that they won't see it in their feeds.

Want to leave a comment on an interesting image on someone's story?

Look at the bottom of your screen while viewing a story and click on the 'write a message' then proceed to type out your message. And if for one reason or the other you want to stop a user from sending you private messages, you can leave them out of people who can send you direct messages.

For a business, this feature lets you create new and interactive live content for your audience. You can have daily challenges, promotions, and other such ideas to keep your social network lively.

2. Live videos

You can have live videos on Instagram. These are a bit tricky as they have no room for editing. They literally stream live as you record them. However, they do provide a great opportunity to promote content.

Take event organizers for instance. They have an opening to further promote their event, hype it up to have people excited about it. They can have live videos of behind the scenes clips, showing the preparations, exclusive interviews and such.

Posting these on Instagram would make the viewers more interested in going to the event, as well as creating an interactive atmosphere for them.

The video doesn't have to be perfect. If the message is passed, then it has served its purpose. Furthermore, you are given the option of saving or discarding it once you finish making it. If you don't like how it sounds, you can always do away with it afterward.

Sharing live videos tends to create a bond with you and the viewers of the video. Of course, it will all depend on your creativity and relevance. Share something that is interesting, entertaining or educative. Take advantage of this feature to improve your account stats.

3. Instagram Algorithm

The aim of Instagram is to have you on their app if possible. This explains the algorithms, which are essentially a way to have only relevant content appearing on your newsfeed.

Picture that boy trying to woo a girl, he would pay attention to her and notice the small details, then he would bring her favorite flowers to her or buy her the ice cream she loves most.

Similarly, Instagram finds out which posts a user wants to see more and brings these to them. The relevance of this content is determined by a user's previous activity in the app, such as posts they have liked, commented on and saved.

The feature is great for your business account as it gives you a greater chance to have your posts viewed despite the time they are posted.

You will need to present your posts in such a way that other users engage with them frequently; have the algorithm work to your advantage. This way, the posts will appear top on the newsfeeds of your followers to ensure that people are liking and commenting on more of your posts.

Have high-quality content that is relevant and engaging, to attract their attention. Also post frequently so they don't forget about your account. Go to your Instagram Insights page to see how different posts perform and get to know which sort of posts to stick to.

There is a lot more you can do to increase the chances of users liking your content. Keep posted for more tips.

4. Instagram Collections

This must have been by far the very best addition yet to Instagram. Picture this: You are scrolling through images on the app, and you come across one of a restaurant that looks wonderful. You promise yourself that you will go there and then move on to other images.

Fast forward to a few weeks later when you want to go to that restaurant but cannot remember:

- Who posted it
- What it is called
- Where it is.

There is no way of finding out other than scrolling through weeks' worth of images to find it.

The user who bumps into your page and later wants to show it to a friend, this is what they would have been forced to do before Instagram introduced the collections feature. It lets a user save posts to a collection. The user can also sort the saved posts and have different topics for several types of posts.

Encourage your followers to save your posts and share with friends later. You can get creative with this to ensure they remember this option and that way you won't lose potential clients to forgetfulness.

You will not be notified when a user saves your post to a collection. Saved videos or images are saved to a private tab that only the user can see and access.

Managing your Account

Photos you are tagged in

While creating your brand, there are things that you may want to be associated with and others not so much. Sometimes, however, it still happens that you are tagged in a photo that you would rather not have associated with your brand.

If you find yourself in such a situation, you may hide the photos or videos you are tagged in. Go to the photos you have been tagged in, click on the three dots on the top right corner and change the options as desired.

You can have the photos you are tagged in to appear on the 'photos of you' section automatically or choose manually which photos appear and which ones do not.

It is advisable to keep tabs on the photos you re tagged in, especially if you have the photos open for public viewing and not hidden.

Push Notifications

You can have the push notifications either on or off for different users that you follow. Turning on push notifications means that you will get notified each time they post something new.

To turn it on, go to the three dots that appear on the profile of a user and select 'Turn on push notifications'.

For your business account, you may not really be interested in being notified when another user posts something. However, you do want your audience to get such a notification.

Are you about to launch a new product? Have a promotion running, or an exciting deal where some of the items are going or a discounted price? Having people turn on the push notifications on Instagram would give you a platform to communicate with potential clients. When you post about it, users will be notified of it.

It reduces chances of missing the post, ensuring the users see the post, and they may even share it with friends and family, further widening your reach. The push notifications feature increases your visibility and keeps you relevant in your circles.

Publishing Images and videos

Custom Stickers

This is another exciting feature on Instagram that brings it closer to Snapchat in terms of similarity. It is new but interesting. If you like to take selfies, this feature should be interesting for you.

While uploading your story, you will see the new option to add a GIF. Tap on it to bring you all these cool moving stickers that you can add to your photo or video to make it more interesting.

There are also the hashtag stickers, another new addition on Instagram that takes hashtags to the next level. You can place a larger font of the hashtag on the image, to make it pop out more.

This is great for both personal accounts and business accounts. You can promote a hashtag more easily with this feature, by placing it in such a way that it is hard to miss.

The hashtag also enables you to appear on other people's, explore pages making you more visible to even more users. Become popular within your network by using this new feature.

You may promote your brand using this feature. Just have the slogan or logo as a hashtag and use this hard-to-miss hashtag which will stick to the memories of users. If it looks cool enough for the users, they may even take it up and use it in their posts which leads to free marketing for you.

Adding the hashtag sticker is also quite straightforward. Once you have chosen the image you wish to post, click on the hashtag in a white box and key in your desired tag, place it where you want and then proceed to post. There you have it, your hard-to-miss hashtag.

Multiple Photos Post

There was a time not so long ago when you could only post one image or video per post on Instagram that time is long gone. Today, you can post multiple photos in a single post. So, when you take photos of products like similar bags in assorted colors, you can have them all in one post.

This feature saves your time and effort as well as that of the viewer. They will only need to swipe left and see the images. You can have images with the same concept together for greater ease of navigation.

Click on the plus sign, to begin with then tap on 'add multiple' on the bottom right. Choose the photos you want to post and then post them all at once.

Cover Thumbnail for Video

When you are posting videos on Instagram, you do it with the hope that it will have multiple views. You want to come back to a ridiculously high number of views. One thing that determines how many people watch your video is the video thumbnail.

The thumbnail tells a user what to expect from the video. Sometimes the very first second of your video may not really make a user feel the need to watch the video.

Maybe there is a specific shot that you are sure will create interest in the viewers. Instagram has got your back on this. You can change your cover shot and pick any frame from your video.

To change the cover shot, first, pick a video you would like to share. Go to the square icon and then use the bottom slider to pick the exact shot you would like to represent your video in. Pick one that is sure to have more people clicking to watch your video.

Multiple Instagram accounts

Yes, you can have multiple Instagram accounts. Have a business account and a personal account, or several business accounts, and switch between them easily with this feature.

You do not have to log out of one first and then log in to the other account; you can save loads of your time now.

How? You might ask.

Follow these steps:

- Go to your profile.

- Click on the three dots in the top right corner. This should bring you to a menu with several options.

- Choose the 'add account' option.

- Follow the prompts to add your account successfully.

- Once your account is added, you can now switch between the accounts by clicking on the username on your profile. It is that fast and easy. You can have a maximum of 5 accounts. Open different accounts accordingly for your brand and manage them all easily.

Instagram keeps changing, and there are already prospects of more changes that will be made soon. To market your products successfully on Instagram, you will need to keep up with the changes.

There may be more opportunities to improve the impact your social media accounts have on your business, and you wouldn't want to miss out on them.

Link up your Instagram account with your other sites as well, such as Facebook, Twitter, and any websites if available. They will complement each other and can have collectively a larger audience than when they are separated.

There are many more features on Instagram apart from the ones mentioned here that serve to make the app what it is today. You can try out different things as you discover new ways of using the app for your benefit. Find what works for you and what does not.

Chapter 3: How to Use Instagram for Marketing and to Earn Money

Instagram today has over 800 million users. Its popularity with the population internationally means that there are many people using it at any given time. This makes it a great avenue for marketing.

Think about it; millions of users, all brought together by the social network, all potential clients for your business. What's better is that you can engage them in the app, and market your product or service to a large audience. You could reach unimaginable heights with your business on Instagram.

Did you know that you can also make money from Instagram?

You do not even have to be a professional marketer with papers to prove it. With a substantial following and the right moves, you could be on your way to making good money with Instagram marketing. Affiliate marketing needs some effort and knowledge of how to get the best out of it.

Whether you are a business owner or affiliate marketer, there is something for each of you here. Let's look at the strategies you should put in place as well as tips on how to improve your skill.

How to Make Money on Instagram

If you are a frequent user of Instagram, then you should think of monetizing your account. Earn some cash while doing what you like to do. Here are a few tips to have you on your way to making money.

Grow your following

The very first step you need to take to start making money on Instagram is to grow your following. It is a requirement of the trade, and the more you have the better for you.

Your following is what you sell to the people you want to pay you. They need to know that they can have a large audience to show their product to, and this is where you come in.

To increase your following, there are a few things you will need to ensure that you;

Have great quality content

This means the images and videos you post need to be of excellent quality. They should be relevant to the field you are interested in. For instance, if you are in the field of sports, then have sports-related content that is educative, entertaining and visually attractive.

People tend to follow accounts with interesting posts, with the aim of seeing more of them so this should be your goal; to attract and keep people's interests.

Make use of shout-outs from other accounts

If you have used Instagram before, then you have seen people getting shout-outs from other users' accounts. That 'Follow my friend's account' message under a user's post is popular.

To get the most out of this, find a relevant user who has a good following. You may have friends or acquaintances that you can ask to give you a shout out and send some of their followers your way, especially on a post that is in your field.

Other than acquaintances, you can also find popular Instagram personalities that give shout outs frequently. Approach them to share your content and mention your username. People who view this content may take interest in your profile and visit it for more posts, possibly even following you to keep updated if they like it.

In case you have no acquaintances with a high following, you can always pay to get shout outs. To do this, you will need to identify a high-ranking influencer, preferably one who has very many followers and high engagement levels, preferably in your niche or at least closely related, for best results.

Next, you will approach the user to endorse your page by mentioning your username and asking his or her followers to check out your account.

Be Consistent

To gain more followers, while you ask for shout outs and create excellent quality content, you need to be consistent with your posts. This means posting frequently and maintaining the quality of your posts throughout.

Posting once and then never going back for a month or two is no way to gain followers. On the contrary, they will 'un-follow' you if you do not show them what made them follow you in the first place.

Use Hashtags

Using relevant hashtags makes you more discoverable, giving more people a chance to follow you. Hashtags put you on the map. When users search for hashtags, they should be able to find your posts. This requires you to have well-tailored hashtags that are easy to find, and more likely to be searched for.

Find Brands to Partner with

Once you have a substantial following, you can now start looking for brands that will work with you. Remember the money needs to come from somewhere. These brands are what will pay to make use of your audience or your posts.

How many followers do you need? You might ask, well the more the merrier.

To start with, try to get at least 5000 followers. Already have more than 5000 followers? If your followers are in the hundreds of thousands or close to a million, then you probably do not need to find brands to partner with as they must have already approached you.

Where to look

You may have several brands in mind that you would like to partner with. You may approach them with your proposal and maybe they will agree to work with you. Keep in mind that larger brands may require a more influential Instagram user. But there are so many brands that would be willing to work with you.

If you have no idea where to start, we have great news for you. You can always join influencer networks. These tend to act as intermediaries and can link you up with potential brands. You as the influencer with a solid following will relate to brands that need such influencers as yourself.

These platforms for you to network in include; Tribe, Buzzweb, and Influence.co among others. They all offer different networking opportunities for you.

Some are good for you if you have a few thousand followers like Tribe. There you just look for brands to work with, create posts for the brand and submit them. If they approve of it you will get paid quickly.

For more than 5000 followers, try out Buzzweb where you can join many campaigns at once and get paid for all of them.

Depending on the network you join, you may get one that calculates potential monthly earning for you depending on your followers. Other networks have brands that pay according to how much traffic your content drives, the people who like and comment or share.

Ways of earning Revenue

There are different paths you can take with earning money on Instagram. You can either earn directly or indirectly. Direct earning is from selling photos you post, or getting payments for tagging companies, posting their products or posts on their page for your audience to see.

The direct ways are simple where you get money for your audience's attention, or for photos that generated a lot of interaction on your profile. It is a quick way of earning money.

Indirect ways of earning from Instagram include driving traffic to the product of the specified brand, or a website, after which you get paid for traffic driven.

You can also earn from Instagram through affiliate marketing. With this, you can use the account to drive traffic to your website. Alternatively, you also have the option of using the account as a page to advertise on.

Therefore, you can post advertisements there for the audience to see, and any interested parties would come forward and ask for information on your comment section or through private messaging.

To drive traffic to a website, you can have a link to your account. Instagram allows a user to add a link on their bio section.

So, if you have a blog, for example, you can ask the viewers on your Instagram page to click on the link on your bio and get access to content on the site it links to.

Other than on your bio, you can add your link on posts, where you place it together with a caption. This is a great way to drive traffic to a website, and generally to advertise a brand and earn money for it.

Finally, you can have images that are relevant to different niches. There are hundreds of stock image sites where you can sell the images you have. Search for such sites on Google and you will find them. To get images that you can sell, you will need to be very creative.

You also need to look for popular niches to base your images on for a higher chance of having your images bought.

Tips to earn well on Instagram

Use hashtags effectively

Have followers relevant to your niche and what you are all about. Followers interested in what you must show are more beneficial than followers who are only there to add to your followers' list.

Engage your audience. Ask for feedback and encourage commenting. More engagement levels lift you up in the eyes of potential partner brands, so you may end up earning more.

Try to keep your identity. You should try not to deviate from what your Instagram page is all about. As such, find brands that are close to your field to remain relevant for longer. This determines your image and affects future partnerships.

Buying Followers

You may have heard of the concept of buying followers. It is a quick way to increase your following. With the high demand for many followers, there has been an increase in hacks to cheat your way out of acquiring followers the traditional way.

There are follower apps, generators, and other such hacks that can multiply your follower count. You may want to go to such lengths to make your account look more lucrative. But is it beneficial in the long run?

These followers that are bought or generated in such ways mentioned above are usually fake. The additional followers may not exist but are powered by bots. Now, this creates quite a problem for you in terms of engagement.

Fake accounts cannot engage with your posts. They can't like or comment on your post. The lack of engagement will have negative impacts on your account. If your analytics are not as good as expected, potential partners may choose to go with a different influencer and you would lose chances to earn from your account.

Put in the work in getting genuine followers, and improving your engagement levels, and you will be on the right path.

How to Use Instagram for Marketing

Instagram's popularity makes it a great platform for marketing. It has a large user base and its rates of engagement are quite high. This creates a great environment for marketing purposes.

Instagram can be quite complicated for a business owner. Where do you start? How do you start to engage your audience? And most importantly, how do you translate that into sales?

There are ways that you can use the app to market your business and grow your brand. We have put together strategies that you may use to connect with the viewers and to ensure that you reach the target market through Instagram.

Maximize the use of hashtags

Hashtags happen to be a crucial factor for Instagram marketing success. They tend to put you on the map to people outside of your followers.

When a user searches for something that is within your field, you want them to be exposed to your posts.

General hashtags

These are easy to find. They are the ones a user is most likely to look for and are sure to drive users to your posts. You can have popular hashtags that have been used a lot like #family, #tbt which will drive a lot of traffic to your account.

While adding these, ensure they are related to your posts, but general enough for easy finding.

Content hashtags

To get more targeted traffic, you can have hashtags that although they are less frequently used, will attract people who want something specific. These are more content-specific and less popular.

They should describe what you offer, so one gets exactly what they wanted when they searched that hashtag. They are more likely to convert into sales.

Brand hashtags

You can also use hashtags to promote your brand by using your company name or a slogan that you associate with your brand. This will put you in the minds of other users.

If you get people to use the slogan, you can gain good marketing from other users, and make your brand stronger.

You can also use hashtags designed to bring more followers specifically like #follow. These hashtags can be used together, you can have several hashtags in a single post and they will all attract different users.

Since there is no limit on the number of hashtags to use, mix them up, using several of them to get more people seeing your page. However, be careful not to look too tacky or desperate by overdoing the hashtags.

Build and be involved in an Instagram Community

Every business owner knows the importance of good customer relationships, and that they are the key to the success of a business. Similarly, you need to nurture good relationships with Instagram users to keep them engaged.

To create a relationship with the users, you can follow them, like and comment on their posts. They may feel the need to reciprocate and follow back. When users leave comments on your posts, reply to the comments to keep the conversation flowing.

Start conversations such as by asking questions or using humor. Make the users feel like they are your friend. An example would be posting an image with the question "What are you having for breakfast this morning," As a way to spark conversation beyond you selling your product or service.

Post more about what your company has been up to. If you had an event, post photos of the event, maybe even have some employees' photos on there to make the account more human.

If users feel they can relate to you, they may be more skewed towards using your brand and telling people about it. Make them feel like they are part of the community.

Use Sponsored Ads

Sponsored Ads are those posts that appear in your newsfeed advertising something. Such posts are very advantageous for you, so they can be shown to users who are not following you.

If the user fits your target audience, you can show your ad on their newsfeed.

More and more businesses are using sponsored ads to get a larger reach for their marketing campaigns. You will be required to part with some of your cash to have a sponsored ad, but you can set an ad budget to keep from using too much money.

Have interesting content that is tailored to the target audience depending on their demographics. If there is a specific post that did extremely well in terms of user engagement, then why not use it on your sponsored ad?

Depending on the audience, you can have different content for the sponsored ads, all running at the same time. This will cater to more people. You can also have photos, videos, Instagram stories or carousel on your sponsored ad, as you please.

Keep Track of your Metrics

The performance of your Instagram determines your next steps. It also tells you how successful different moves are and where there is room for improvements. The metrics that you need to keep track of include:

Follower Growth

You need to keep adding followers. If your followers are not increasing, then that might point to a problem. The total number of followers may not be as important as how many new followers you have gotten over a specific period. Having low follower growth rate tells you to change your strategy to increase followers, so keep track of this.

Engagement rate

Are the users engaging with you? Are the likes and comments increasing or not? You should be more precise by looking at the level of engagement brought by different posts. You may get a pattern and find posts that people seem to favor over others and have more similar content to post.

Click through rate of URLs

You can tell how many people are clicking on the link on your bio. If the number is extremely low, then it might be time to change your tactics and find better ways to bring traffic to click on that link.

Such metrics keep you on your toes. You get to know which strategies are working and which are not. You also understand your audience and what they like, all of which are required to be more effective on Instagram.

Partner with Influencers

Sometimes you may need some bit of help with getting your brand out there. One strategy that is sure to work is working with influencers in your industry.

These are people with a large following of users who trust recommendations they make. The influencers tend to have a wide reach as well as the trust of the people. This is important for a new brand that is just starting out as people may not trust it.

The influencers will help get your brand to users, they may give a shout out on their accounts or post your products for their followers to see, maybe even promote an event or contest that you plan to hold.

You will need to choose an influencer who is relevant in your field, to generate traffic that is more targeted.

Also, think of a more long-term step with the influencer as compared to short-term efforts. You can make use of the attention from their audience to launch several campaigns over a period of time.

Create more awareness for your brand like this.

Hold Contests

People love competitions. You can hold contests and have giveaways to increase engagement and have people talking about your brand. These require your creativity. It needs to be something interesting that people will want to do.

The most popular contest on Instagram is the image contest that can be presented in different ways. For instance, having them share a specific image on their account with a hashtag generated by you. The one with the most likes on that image wins the contest.

Such contests are good as they help you have more viewers seeing your brand and possibly more followers.

Consider User-submitted photos

Collection of user-submitted photos is a great way to kill two birds with one stone. Increase user-generation and get content to post on your account while you are at it.

You can get the people to submit photos by holding a contest of some sort, where the most creative gets featured on your account. In return, you can offer to tag them in the post.

Of course, while choosing the photos to post, ensure that they are most beneficial to you.

The photos should:

- Fit with your brand
- Be from a user with a substantial following
- Be appropriate
- Be relevant to your field

Be consistent in your posts

You will need to post frequently to remain relevant. However, refrain from posting too frequently. If all your followers see are posts from your account, they will un-follow you to keep from seeing too much of your posts.

If you find problems posting, you can always opt for the pre-scheduled posts which you choose in advance and have them posted at the designated times each day without you having to post them every other day.

Instagram marketing is best done with a business account, as it has more tools and gives you more insights. There is no specific method to have a sure win with Instagram marketing.

You can, however, use the tips given to improve results. Just try out different techniques finding which works best for your business using the strategies mentioned to guide you.

Use Instagram marketing, together with other social media marketing, to grow your brand and increase sales or get into affiliate marketing to earn from your Instagram account.

Chapter 4: Instagram Success Stories

Digital marketing has become a requirement for the success of any business today because a majority of people are online.

We have looked at the use of social media, specifically Instagram. We have gone through its features and how you can use them for the benefit of your business. Yet all this is in theory.

How can you be assured of the success of Instagram marketing?

We have compiled a few success stories. These are in business like you and have employed the use of Instagram in their marketing. They have tried and tested the app and have had success beyond measure.

Read on to hear of actual brands and businesses which have used Instagram; some relying on it for all marketing purposes and shunning traditional marketing and succeeding because of it.

Anish Bhatt

Anish Bhatt was fired from his job in the fashion industry at age 29 in the US. This led to his going back to London where he had grown up. He felt dejected, having lost his source of income. He had to start all over again.

Normally, losing your job takes a toll on you. You may suffer from depression, and struggle to get back on your feet. You may even give up completely and just go with the flow, settle for something less.

For Anish, this was nowhere in his plan. Instead of relaxing and feeling bad for himself and about his situation, he decided to do something about it. He had an eye for fashion, watches. His interest in watches formed the basis for his next work.

Instead of going for something like what he had done before, he decided to try a different path. He put together his vast knowledge in watches and interest in photography to build his brand and make it what it is today.

Anish Bhatt did not use traditional marketing at all. The brand has been promoted only through digital marketing. He started off as one man with a passion for watches and photography, putting in a lot of challenging work, time and commitment. He grew his following slowly from scratch with his amazing images.

If he started out so simply, then how did he get to more than 1.6 million followers?

He did not use bots or other hacks that people have used. What Anish did was that he was very engaging with other Instagram users. He would like and comment on images that appealed to him constantly. He followed other users.

It was not just him posting images on his account and waiting for other users to notice him. He put himself out there by taking an interest in other popular accounts. This made him known to others, and the users returned his gesture. Slowly, he built his list of followers.

He also took his time to come up with amazing images to post on his feed. He created a brand that set him apart from the rest, through his images of watches. He sells the kind of lifestyle that is lived by billionaires. His images give you the feeling that the watches make you look and feel like the very distinguished person that you are.

He chose luxurious backgrounds like hotels, exotic cars and private jets, the kind of life that very few can afford, yet everyone wants. He was not just promoting watches, but a lifestyle. This attracted his followers. He grew slowly to his current level and brought together a team of people to work with.

If you look at his page today, it looks very elegant and classy, far from the social media publication that it is. He has grown into a very popular brand.

He has and continues to travel the world to exotic destinations, where he develops the photos for different brands of watches like Rolex. You will find photos from places like Dubai, Paris and such places all part of his aim of presenting a much sought-after lifestyle. Watch brands seek him to promote their products when they want to further their reach past geographical and even social boundaries like class.

As impossible as it may sound, Anish has been able to build a publication that is solely digital for watches, which has turned into a multi-million-dollar business.

Reebok

Reebok is well known for its sports attire. You must have seen a pair of sports shoes with the 'Reebok' label. It has also been running successful campaigns of its products through social media, and especially on Instagram.

The brand has used diverse types of image content in its Instagram feed, all aimed at achieving the different capabilities of Instagram.

Its action shots, that is, photos that show the product in use, tend to motivate one to go out for a run. They are set up in a way that shows the product in a real-life setting; for instance, a fit, healthy man running in his 'Reebok' shoes. They are inspiring, and they make one want to exercise more regularly.

They also make use of user-generated photos and product photos, bringing to the viewers a variety. The viewers are therefore engaged in different ways.

Their regular posts keep them relevant to Instagram users. Having images that show your products in the real world helps the viewers see the use of the product and why they would need it in their lives while making your brand more credible.

J Crew

This is one brand that has been successful in its Instagram marketing. It has a very attractive feed that draws one to it. It markets itself as a lifestyle brand by having assorted images of people, flowers, and quotes. It encompasses a lot of the various aspects of daily life in its feed.

It also tends to show user-generated photos. This move is a smart one on their part, as it makes the audience feel like they are part of the brand. It is also a way of appreciating the audience for their time and effort in engaging with the account.

These user-generated tend to benefit both the audience and the business. A user whose photo is featured gets a shout out which would increase their following and presence. Such an image also works for the company by acting as a form of testimonial for a newer audience, increasing trust.

J Crew also tends to use the Instagram stories feature to further their promotion tactics. The feature is especially good for introducing a new product to your audience. They had, for instance, held a promotion of a new pair of sunglasses by them that they pushed through Instagram stories. They had an offer for the sunglasses which they mentioned in their story.

Check out the screenshots of their Instagram stories promotion, which was a simple, bright collection of images and words explaining the offer.

Figure 1: Snapshot J Crew Instagram Story (Copyright by J Crew, https://www.jcrew.com/)

Figure 2: Snapshot J Crew Instagram Story (Copyright by J Crew, https://www.jcrew.com/)

Figure 3: Snapshot J Crew Instagram Story (Copyright by J Crew, https://www.jcrew.com/)

Figure 4: Snapshot J Crew Instagram Story (Copyright by J Crew, https://www.jcrew.com/)

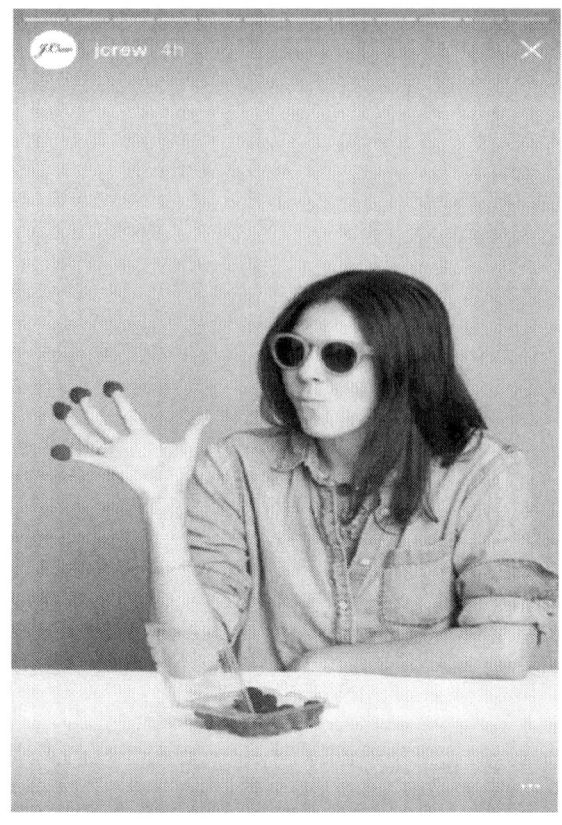

Figure 5: Snapshot J Crew Instagram Story (Copyright by J Crew, https://www.jcrew.com/)

Figure 6: Snapshot J Crew Instagram Story (Copyright by J Crew: https://www.jcrew.com/)

Note how they use a similar background color to keep with the color scheme. It is all very simple with not too many things going on in one photo so as not to take away from the main message.

The color appeals to its target market which is the young females. The images are fun and show the sunglasses in use in the real world, as you can even see how one would look while wearing them. The campaign led to quite successful sales.

@spjeweler

This account belongs to Sean Perelstein, the CEO of Sting HD. The company is a jewelry design company that is very high-end, and designs jewelry from high-grade leather from pythons, alligators and such, together with precious metals and jewels.

It is based in New York and is highly exclusive, its client base including prominent people and celebrities internationally.

Today it is known worldwide, yet this was not so only a few years ago.

In fact, Perelstein was only introduced to social media by a friend while Instagram was still new. He began to take photos of his jewelry pieces together with luxury watches and posting on Instagram.

His images drew attention from people worldwide. He sold a lifestyle that was very indulgent by giving his jewelry ideal settings. He made sales through social media including his first sale.

He met his business partner, Chase Zimmerman through the sales and they worked together. This was how they grew, through digital marketing.

The company has worked with major partners like Saks Fifth Avenue Stores all over the world, with its pieces going for several hundred dollars, up to more than 100,000 dollars each.

Perelstein made use of hashtags to further promote his business. He took photos with luxury brands like Cartier and shared them on his feed adding relevant hashtags together with his to get Instagram users who were interested in such a lifestyle to know his brand.

It worked wonders, increasing his audience and making his Instagram page successful.

Hunter Vought

The man behind the @VoTrends account is another testimony to the power of Instagram Marketing. He has a keen attention to detail and uses this in his ideas in men's wear.

He runs a fashion account featuring menswear, to which he grew a following very fast. He gained 50,000 followers in about 3 to 4 months in 2016. By September of that year, he had already reached the 100,000 followers' mark.

He also went ahead to use this fashion account to market his own personal brand, thus becoming an influencer. This move was a very clever one as it further increases his abilities on Instagram.

He is not only a business person marketing his product but now has the potential to start earning on Instagram by partnering with other brands.

Slowly, Hunter has grown his personal brand and his name and continues to grow it so as to make himself stand out from the rest. People are bound to notice and will want to work with him, have him promote their product.

Pacific Northwest Wonderland

This company used the short story feature to launch a successful Instagram Campaign. They were launching a promotion that would be there for a short time.

Such a technique worked well because of the disappearing factor of Instagram Stories, where they vanish after 24 hours. This is perfect for a promotion that you would like to run for a day or so.

Placing the promotions on the normal newsfeeds would mean that you cannot get rid of it without deleting. Of course, it also reaches the people who follow your story.

This company, for instance, had people click on the link on their bio. Having the promotion on the stories feature meant that more users would see it as it appeared on top of one's newsfeed.

Use of the Instagram stories feature for limited promotion was successful for the company because of people's love for promotions.

Figure 7: Snapshot from Pacific Northwest Wonderland Instagram Story (Copyright by Pacific Northwest Wonderland, https://pnwonderland.com/)

E! News

E! News has been able to successfully promote content on Instagram. This is quite different from promoting products. Remember there is no actual product, just trying to encourage the audience to read their magazine or watch their show.

They market their brand by posting on Instagram Stories some headlines from their magazines. It is a great way to tell the audience what they can expect and present it in a way that will make the user want to get themselves a copy of the newspapers instantly.

The strategy also makes users who view it start a conversation on the same, by maybe commenting, which then increases engagement for the users. The posts also keep them relevant to their audience; no risk of them being forgotten.

We can pick out very many success stories; we could go on and on about the very many businesses that have had successful Instagram marketing, and continue to thrive off it. What appears in most of them, especially for those just starting out, is the need to be consistent.

The strategy will not work out overnight, nor will it come easy. Like most things, it requires hard work, effort and time, before it kicks off. Yet it is worth the wait as your sales shoot up later when you make progress with it.

Keep at it, put in place the strategies we talked about in chapter 3 and you will be on your way to making your own success story.

Chapter 5: Importance of Instagram for Online Business Success

Instagram is one of the best tools for promoting your business today. Whatever the size of your business, whether it's an established business or you are just starting out or even when what you want to promote is your own personal brand; Instagram is a tool you just can't ignore if you want to further your business reach.

Benefits of using Instagram for marketing

There are many advantages of using Instagram for your marketing purposes. It provides chances for your business and avenues that you might not have gotten with any other strategies. Let's look at some of those benefits.

Visual appeal

The very essence of Instagram is the visual appeal. The network is all about images and videos that appeal to its audience. You can communicate with your audience through images, which are better in the long run than written content.

Photos tend to encourage more engagement than written content. It is easier for the audience to see and understand and takes much less of their time.

Instagram also lets you test out different forms of images and find out which one's appeal most to the audience. You can then use these on other channels such as your website or blog and email newsletters. The photo sharing ability for Instagram enables you to showcase your product in a creative manner.

If you can come up with great content for your Instagram feed, it could change your whole business and increase sales for you in the long run.

Large Audience

Instagram provides you with an extremely large audience who are also potential clients. With over 150 million active users, it gives a rather impressive possibility for your business. Imagine that, being able to market your business to millions of people all at once.

It is easier than traditional marketing where the audience can see your photos at once. Compare it to a billboard you put up where only people who drive by the area can see it, and only those not distracted by one thing or the other.

Instagram on the other hand allows your audience to view the image and they can hardly miss it on their feed. They are also not limited by geographic location or time.

The app is also great for when you are expanding to branches across the world, as it has users all over the world. This allows you to market internationally, with just one marketing campaign. You can do it all from a central location without ever having stepped in some of the areas your audience is from.

The use of hash tags allows you to increase your audience, as more people can access your content through the hash tag.

More Engagement

Instagram has quite a high engagement rate. When running a marketing campaign, you want your audience to be as engaging as possible, at that moment and in future too.

To generate engagement on Instagram is quite easy as all you would need is to follow those people who talk about your brand, comment on and like another users' content. Using hash tags also allows you to facilitate conversation. You can have the users contribute to a topic by asking a question.

The community you build on Instagram is likely to engage more often because they will see your content regularly. Unlike a post on a blog where they must go to your blog to see additional content,

Instagram lets your followers see content by you on their feed if they are already on the app.

Such constant engagement ensures that your customers will come back for repeat purchases. That when one buys from your brand, and they see it again several times, the next time they need something that you offer, they will most likely buy from your brand again.

Increased engagement also makes it easier to introduce new products to your audience.

Storytelling Ability

Creating your brand on Instagram can take up different forms. The app allows you to create a story behind your products. Through posts on the stories feature, you can show your audience some behind-the –scenes images and videos. Have them relate to your brand by introducing your staff and maybe even yourself to them.

You can also have images that show your clients the products in real life situations, create a lifestyle with your brand. Tell the audience a story through the different Instagram features.

Keep Tabs on Competition

Instagram gives you the ability to see what other businesses in your industry are doing. By following the hash tags that are like your own will show you how the others in the industry are promoting their brands.

Get ideas from them on how better to market your products and stay ahead.

Free Marketing from users

This is the ideal kind of marketing that any business would love to have. It is made possible by Instagram through User Generated Content. Remember that your audience is also creating and sharing content of their own.

If you post user generated content, you may be able to tap into a different audience other than those who follow you. It is also a great way to connect with your audience and interact even more.

By having the users add a hash tag generated by you to their posts, they market your business and in return, you can pick one of their posts to add to your feed and give them a shout out.

There are many more benefits to using Instagram for marketing, all of which you will gain once you start using the medium.

Tips for successful Instagram marketing

There are ways that you can gain from all the benefits that Instagram offers. Some of these ways include:

Having a Great Profile

Your Instagram profile shows people who you are. By getting it right, you make yourself that much more appealing to your clients. Include contacts on your profile, which is possible with a business account.

From your user name to your bio, links and anything else on your profile, make it stand out. Also update it frequently, to avoid misrepresentation.

Offering excellent quality Content

Since Instagram is all about sharing visual images, you will need to ensure that your photos and videos are of excellent quality and creative. This sets you apart from the rest of the Instagram community, and attracts users to your feed.

Stay away from shabby photos and ensure the content represents your brand accordingly.

Being Consistent

Once you have excellent quality content, you also need to ensure that you are consistent with posting, and with the overall look of your profile. The color scheme of your feed should also be consistent, as it forms part of your brand and allows easier recognition from your followers.

Try to come up with a style that is unique to your business and stick to that style. This should include hash tags, color scheme, times of posting and such. Consistency makes your brand look more appealing to the audience.

Increasing User Engagement

This is one of the most important tips for great Instagram marketing. Optimizing user engagement lets you get more out of your account. You will need to use every technique possible to make sure that people are engaging with your posts.

Get people talking about your brand; whatever steps you take, ensure that you take the time to really engage with your audience.

When they leave comments, ensure that you respond to them, answer their questions, and you can simply tell them 'thank you'. Putting in effort makes the audience like your brand more, as they can relate with you. Do not take weeks to reply to questions asked; be as quick as possible to maintain a good reputation.

For any complaints that may be aired on the comment section, try to direct the ones who make the complaint to direct message so that you can try and assist them better privately.

Also follow other users, like some of their posts and comment on them to further your engagement. And when you post photos, encourage the audience to leave comments on the posts.

Holding contests is another way of encouraging user engagement. These will also give you user generated content to post on your feed and allow testimonials from your followers who take part in your contests.

Influencer Marketing

This has gained traction over the years. You could incorporate it into your marketing strategy and further promote your brand in this manner.

By finding an Instagram account that has a lot of influence over many users, you could partner with them and pay them to market your products. You will need to find an influencer that has an audience you wish to target, that is preferably one in the same industry as you.

Influencer marketing gives you many people at your disposal to share information about your brand with and may increase your following as more users know of your existence through the influencers.

Furthermore, influencers tend to have an impact on the audience's choices. Having one promote your brand creates more trust for the user than if it was just you appealing to them.

Utilizing Instagram Ads

Instagram ads are a fantastic way to market your business if done correctly. They are made even better by the chance you have of targeting a specific audience based on geographic location, interests and such dynamics.

It does cost you, but the benefits far outweigh the costs in this case. Get your ad seen by users who do not follow you but fit your target description.

These are just a few tips to get you going on your efforts to use Instagram for marketing. There are very many techniques that you can use, but with these tips and a will to succeed, you will be on your way to actual success in just a short while.

Conclusion

We have been through a journey of discovery of Instagram; what it is, its uses, and benefits for your business.

We have seen the features if Instagram, its functionalities as well as strategies that you can use to further improve your Instagram marketing campaigns. These will set you off in the right direction and propel your business to even greater heights.

Instagram is now a required platform to market your business if you want to have a chance at competing with other firms within your niche. It is a proven way to get your name out there to a larger more diverse audience and promote your brand.

Get a business account today to start promoting your brand through Instagram, if you do not already have one. Then start out with the tips given and try out different techniques, having your brand to guide you in terms of color schemes and the kind of content you post.

Do keep in mind that Instagram is not a quick way to multiply sales. You will not open your account today and get results tomorrow. Contrary to that, you will need to put work into it, be patient and keep working on improving your statistics daily. Instagram is made to grow through consistency in your actions.

Slowly, you will start to see changes in your business, an increase in sales, more people reacting to your brand. With time, you might even get free marketing where users share your content themselves and even use your hashtags without you prompting them to. Get more conversions by using Instagram in a smart way.

We hope that you have enjoyed the book and that it has been of assistance to you in understanding how to use Instagram for your marketing needs.

Thank you for downloading this book.

Did you like the book?

I'm happy about your rating, because that really helps me a lot. So, I can either improve something or appreciate that you have read my book and would like to thank you for your time.

Many Thanks.

© Jennifer Hauser

Copyright: 2018

1st Edition

Self-published
Print: Amazon Media EU S.à.r.l., 5 Rue Plaetis, L-2338, Luxembourg
The work including its parts is protected by copyright. Any use is prohibited without the consent of the publisher and the author. This applies to electronic or other duplication, translation, distribution and public disclosure.
Contact: Eugen Grinschuk - Grünauer Allee 14 – 82008 Unterhaching
Cover photo: depositphotos.com

Printed in Poland
by Amazon Fulfillment
Poland Sp. z o.o., Wrocław